Guides to European Decorative Arts, No. 5

This publication was supported by COLLAB
The Contemporary Design Group for the Philadelphia Museum of Art

Design *1900–1940*

Kathryn B. Hiesinger
and George H. Marcus

Philadelphia Museum of Art

Cover: Armchair, 1930–33. Designed by Alvar Aalto (Finnish, 1898–1976). Laminated birch and birch plywood, height 26″ (66 cm). Purchased with funds contributed by COLLAB in honor of Cynthia W. Drayton, and the Fiske Kimball Fund 1985-67-2 (*see* page 36)

Color photography by Eric Mitchell

Library of Congress Cataloging-in-Publication Data

Philadelphia Museum of Art.
Design, 1900–1940.

(Guides to European decorative arts; no. 5)
Bibliography: p.
1. Design—Europe—History—20th century—Catalogs. 2. Decorative arts—Europe—History—20th century—Catalogs. 3. Philadelphia Museum of Art—Catalogs. I. Hiesinger, Kathryn B., 1943– . II. Marcus, George H. III. Title. IV. Series
NK1442.P47 1987 745.4′494
86–30656
ISBN 0–87633–068–5 (pbk.)

The following have provided information from various archival sources: Chantal Bizot and Evelyne Possémé, Musée des Arts Décoratifs, Paris; Britt Blomquist, Orrefors Glasbruk; Benoît Castelli, Puiforcat Orfèvre; Bernard Dunand; Flemming Eskildsen, Royal Copenhagen; Wendy Evans, The Museum of London; Mme Roger Froment; Florence Marinot; Hermann Pyro, Württembergische Metallwarenfabrik; Marja Pystynen, Artek; and Messrs. Schulz and Schärer, VEB Staatliche Porzellan-Manufaktur Meissen. At the Museum Donna Corbin has most ably assisted with research, and P. Andrew Lins and Melissa Meighan have contributed their expertise on technical matters.

Introduction

When in conjunction with the Philadelphia Centennial Exhibition of 1876, the decision was made to found an art museum in the city, one of the goals of the organizers was to collect the finest arts of the day "with a special view to the development of the Art Industries of the State." Outstanding examples of ceramics, glass, metalwork, and furniture were acquired from the wares shown by craftsmen at the Centennial Exhibition, and objects of contemporary manufacture continued to be collected by the new museum. From the great international exhibitions in Paris (1878 and 1900) and Chicago (1893), the Museum bought French and English ceramics and glass, and German and Austrian metalwork, first in historicizing styles and then in the new decorative style of 1900. However, already by the turn of the century, as the emphasis of the Museum expanded to include the fine arts, contemporary decorative arts and design began to be neglected. Not until the late 1960s, through the enthusiasm of Calvin S. Hathaway, then Curator of Decorative Arts, did this area once again become a priority. In the intervening years objects of European design from this century had occasionally been acquired, among the most important being gifts from the families of two French designers, the architect Hector Guimard (in 1948–49) and the glassmaker Maurice Marinot (in 1967). With the founding of COLLAB, the Contemporary Design Group for the Philadelphia Museum of Art, in 1970, the means was established for Philadelphia's design professionals, allied with the Friends of the Museum, to support the Museum's activities in the field of contemporary design. COLLAB has supported research and special exhibitions at the Museum, and its gifts, along with those of many private individuals, have greatly enriched the collections of both the prewar and postwar periods.

Chair, 1902
Peter Behrens (German, 1868–1940)

6 Peter Behrens designed this chair for an exhibition of "modern interiors" at the Wertheim department store in Berlin in 1902, to which several other well-known architects and designers contributed, among them the Germans Richard Riemerschmid and August Endell and the Englishman Hugh Baillie Scott. One critic considered Behrens's dining room "one of the most interesting [interiors] of the whole series. It is a uniform creation where every shape is subject to the intention of an orderly will. . . . A basic rectangular form . . . appears as flat ornament on the walls . . . in the porcelain service, the knotted carpet, and in relief on the silverwares. It takes three-dimensional form and . . . influences the shape of the furniture, the buffet and sideboard . . . as well as the construction of the backrest of the chairs."

Behrens's geometrically systematized interior presented a marked contrast to the dining room of his own house in Darmstadt completed the previous year. There he experimented with the freely curved lines used by the Belgian Art Nouveau designer Henry van de Velde, whose house near Brussels had been widely publicized in Germany. Only in its arched back and waisted legs does this chair recall that earlier style, while its form is defined by the flat rectangular pattern of the pierced crest rail and horizontal stretchers that join splat and back posts. In its embodiment of an abstract geometrical order, the chair anticipates Behrens's work for the Allgemeine Elektrizitäts-Gesellschaft (AEG), where as a pioneer in the practice of industrial design, he conceived not only the buildings but also the products and publicity material of this electric company.

Oak and woven rush
Height 39¼″ (100 cm)
Gift of COLLAB in honor of Elisabeth
L. Fraser. 1981-28-1

Ewers, c. 1903
Württembergische Metallwarenfabrik, Geislingen (established 1853)

8 The Württembergische Metallwarenfabrik (WMF), Germany's largest metalware manufacturer, was founded in 1853 to produce silver-plated tableware. Expanding production rapidly, the firm by the turn of the century had hundreds of workers and several factories, including a glassworks, and its large production enabled it to offer wares suited to many styles of decoration. Suggesting a growing demand for the Art Nouveau style, these silver-plated ewers with curving, plant-derived ornamentation appeared in the WMF catalogues between 1903 and 1912 as model number 258. They are shown there individually set on a tray with six beakers with gilded interiors. The service appears alongside an eclectic variety of comparable sets in metal and in glass as but one of many design choices available for the table, from heavily ornamented, mounted glass goblets and ewers in Renaissance style to the restrained neoclassical lines of cut-glass carafes and undecorated stemware.

These ewers are ornamented with flowing bands in low relief, intertwined below and growing upward; the oak-leaf decoration in openwork in the handles and in relief under the lips is all that remains of recognizable plant motifs. The nervous angularity of the profiles immediately distinguishes these pieces from the delicate, sinuous floral forms of the Art Nouveau in other countries. They demonstrate the more robust, albeit controlled, expressiveness of this style as it developed in Germany, where it was known as Jugendstil.

Plated silver
Marks: (left) as, WMFB, 1, 0, 80, 39 (stamped), N (incised); (right) as, WMFB, 2, 0, 80, 24 (stamped), N (incised)
Height 14 3/16″ (36 cm)

Gift of Mr. and Mrs. Louis Sherman
1979-171-3a,b

Chair, c. 1904
Josef Hoffmann (Austrian, 1870–1956)

10 This chair was designed for the dining room of the sanatorium at Purkersdorf, near Vienna, which between 1904 and 1905 was built and furnished in large part after the designs of Josef Hoffmann. In 1906 the chair appeared in commercial production, published in the sales catalogue of the Jacob & Josef Kohn firm as model number 322, along with a similar table, settee, and armchair. The severely rectilinear character of the chair reflects the design of the room it furnished: a long rectangular hall framed and outlined by straight ceiling beams and slablike wall surfaces, each clearly defined by a narrow, leaf-patterned frieze. In describing the sanatorium and its furnishings, one critic noted that its "chief beauty lies in that due proportion which is so prominent a feature in Professor Hoffmann's works"; another described Hoffmann's "bubbling inventiveness" in adding wooden spheres at the joints of various pieces of his furniture. Hoffmann's concern for cube and rectangle, for rationalized geometric forms became a hallmark of progressive Viennese design of the period.

In an essay of 1901 entitled "Simple Furniture," Hoffmann gave the clarion call for the need for a "modern" style. Taking aim against both historicism and the excesses of Art Nouveau, Hoffmann asked, "Where, in these deprived times shall we find not imitation but a valid tradition?" His answer lay in industrial form, and he criticized museums for not displaying "a beautiful machine." Despite their "due proportion," formal simplicity, and economical structure, Hoffmann's solutions at Purkersdorf were not without a sense of decorative enrichment, the "bubbling inventiveness" of whimsically placed wooden spheres and floral friezes, which persisted in Hoffmann's work long beyond the period of such rigorously simple geometric designs.

Made by Jacob & Josef Kohn, Vienna
(established 1868)
Beech and leather
Height 38⅝″ (98.5 cm)

Purchased: Bloomfield-Moore Fund
69-136-7

Tea Service, 1904
Otto Eduard Voigt (German, 1870–1949)

Formerly attributed to the Belgian designer Henry van de Velde, the "Saxonia Service," to which these pieces belong, has been identified in the records of the Meissen porcelain factory as the work of Otto Eduard Voigt, an artist who came to Meissen in 1896 as a flower painter and remained there until 1932. Van de Velde, an independent designer of international reputation, was brought to Meissen in 1902 to modernize the production of the factory, which had been roundly criticized at the Paris Exposition Universelle of 1900. Van de Velde introduced the fully developed Art Nouveau style he had pioneered, and although he was to design only a single service for the factory (in 1903–4), his influence there was immediate. In the "Saxonia Service" Voigt understood the lessons of van de Velde: the interplay of curved line and empty space creating abstract patterns, the use of streamlined shapes, and the elegant functionalism of tilted handles obliging the user's fingers. Voigt was particularly interested in decorating porcelains with colors that could be fired at high temperatures, a technique that had been developed at Meissen by the 1900 exhibition and was used in the "Saxonia Service" to achieve the deeper tones of blue and gray. After 1904 Voigt continued to experiment with such high-firing colors, painting naturalistic landscape and floral designs on various ornamental wares. The retreat from abstract to naturalistic forms in Voigt's work paralleled the retreat from the bold experiments in the new style at Meissen, where historicizing porcelains continued to dominate the factory's production, and where by 1910 even the van de Velde service could be dismissed as "not at all successful in form . . . not well adapted to china, and . . . more fit for being made in metal."

Made by the Königlich Sächsische Porzellanmanufaktur, Meissen (established 1710)
Hard-paste porcelain with enamel colors
Marks: crossed swords (in underglaze blue); (creamer) U 153 61, (sugar bowl) U 154, (teapot) U 152, (tray) U 128 (incised)
Height (teapot) 6⅛" (15.4 cm)
Gift of the Friends of the Philadelphia Museum of Art. 73-94-5

Tray, 1909
Hector Guimard (French, 1867–1942)

The greatest of French Art Nouveau architect-designers, Hector Guimard designed buildings, ironwork, ceramics, and furniture with equal brilliance. Along with metalwork of domestic scale such as this gilded copper tray, Guimard designed entrances and railings for the Paris Métro stations, his most notable work, and fitted his buildings with cast-iron ornaments ranging from door fittings to balcony cartouches. These were published in 1907 in a catalogue, the *Fontes artistiques . . .* , in which the designs compare closely in style with this tray: a kind of linear sculpture, swift in movement, with swirling curves and wavelike flourishes that suggest natural forms reduced to abstract patterns. He subtitled the catalogue "Style Guimard," which he had earlier defined by stressing analogies with nature while acknowledging practical requirements. In 1902 he wrote, "Nature is a book from which we draw inspiration and it is in that book that we must look for principles, which when found, have to be defined and applied by the human mind according to human needs."

Sometimes Guimard made two versions of the objects he designed: one he would sign, date, and offer for sale; the other, unsigned, he would keep. The gilded-bronze version of this dish, signed and dated "Hector Guimard 1909," was purchased by the Musée des Arts Décoratifs in Paris (inv. 18101) from the Salon des Artistes Décorateurs in 1911. The unsigned version, retained by the artist, came to the Museum from his widow. In 1949 she wrote to Fiske Kimball, then the Museum's director, "These days, I have begun the distribution of the portable objects created by Mr. Guimard. . . . I would very much like to reserve for your Museum a few choice objects . . . an *important* bronze platter—the original is at the Louvre (Pavillon Marsan) bgt. 1911—and, I have the only replica."

Gilded copper
Diameter 8½″ (46.6 cm)
Gift of Mme Hector Guimard. 49-43-1

Goblet, 1908
Harry J. Powell (English, 1853–1922)

16 In 1835 James Powell and Sons took over the Whitefriars Glassworks, London, manufacturers of quality table glass, and made it one of the principal glasshouses of the Arts and Crafts movement. The firm made glass designed by Philip Webb for William Morris, which was sold by Morris and Company from the early 1860s; exhibited regularly in Arts and Crafts exhibitions; and at the turn of the century, supplied glass to Liberty's, in London, and to the progressive Paris shops L'Art Nouveau, of Samuel Bing, and La Maison Moderne, of Julius Meier-Graefe. Harry J. Powell joined his family's firm in 1875 and from 1880 directed production and designed glasswares in historicizing and Art Nouveau styles. Remaining faithful to the principles of the Arts and Crafts movement, which attempted to revive handicrafts and improve standards of design, Powell advocated a return to the methods and materials of sixteenth- and seventeenth-century glassmakers, whose glasses were free blown and decorated in their molten state. Blown from greenish soda-lime glass, this goblet recalls early seventeenth-century precedents in its use of that material and in its form, with knopped stem and furnace-wrought trailed and pincered decoration. The goblet is typical of the Powell glasswares sold by Morris and Company, and in its simple shape, lightness, delicacy, and natural gradation of color, it reflects the virtues of Arts and Crafts design. An early version of this goblet appears in a design book of about 1903 in the Powell archives in the Museum of London. The glass is shown in its present form in a design book of 1907–8 as model number 0 2357 and is recorded there as ordered by the Artificers Guild of London on November 5, 1908, for twenty-five shillings. This guild, a commercial enterprise with a trade in handicraft, survived until the First World War.

Made by James Powell and Sons,
Whitefriars Glassworks, London
(established 1835)
Clear, greenish soda-lime glass and cased gold leaf

Height 7¾" (19.7 cm)
Purchased with funds contributed by
Mr. and Mrs. Stanley Bernstein. 1981-90-1

Armchair, c. 1912
Hector Guimard (French, 1867–1942)

This chair was designed for the dining room of Hector Guimard's house, number 122 avenue Mozart in Paris, which was built by Guimard shortly after his marriage to the American painter Adeline Oppenheim. Executed between 1909 and 1912, the house contained reception and living quarters, Guimard's office suite, and a studio on the third floor for Mme Guimard. The dining room, which occupied one of two oval rooms on the first floor, demonstrated the innovative decorative style for which Guimard was known. Conceived entirely in plant forms and united by soft, flowing curves, the architecture and interior decoration—from plaster ceiling ornaments, lighting fixtures, and door and window hardware to woodwork and furniture—represented an exercise in total design, a single comprehensive aesthetic. This and the other dining chairs were carved with tendril-like crest rails, which appear as if they might sprout and blossom, and were originally ranged around a table whose legs seemed to grow naturalistically out of a mound of carpeting. In an interview of 1899, Guimard described the source of his synthetic style: "It is from nature that one must always seek advice. When I design a piece of furniture or sculpt it, I reflect upon the spectacle the universe provides. Beauty appears there in constant variety. There is no parallelism, no symmetry: forms are perpetuated in movements that are never the same."

After the designer's death, his widow hoped to make their house a Guimard museum. She was later obliged to sell the house, however, and it was subsequently transformed into an apartment building. In 1948–49 she donated furniture and objects from the house to European and American museums; most of the dining-room furnishings were given to the Musée d'Art Moderne in Paris.

Cherry wood and leather
Height 43⅝″ (111.7 cm)
Gift of Mme Hector Guimard. 48-64-1

Secretary, 1921
Emile-Jacques Ruhlmann (French, 1879–1933)

Emile-Jacques Ruhlmann was often compared by his contemporaries to the master cabinetmakers of the eighteenth century, for like them he created veneered and inlaid pieces of rare and costly materials, and he equaled them in the meticulous craftsmanship he demanded. A designer, not a craftsman, Ruhlmann employed a staff of architects and draftsmen to translate his quick sketches into elevations, plans, and full-scale working drawings for his cabinetmakers, who until 1923 were outside contractors. Despite the comparison with earlier cabinetmakers, when he did open his own workshops he took a modern approach. "I work on the principle," he is quoted as saying, "that nothing that can be done by machine should be done by hand. Modern furniture has little ornamentation and consists almost entirely of flat surfaces veneered with precious woods. Machines make it easier to do the preparatory work." Even with machines, his workmen devoted months to the completion of each piece, and he supervised the production of each one himself. The care given to his manufacture is apparent in the perfectly matched graining of the ebony veneer of this secretary and in the delicate inlays of ivory, which define the form of its tapering, concave front legs and enhance its top with classical dentil and volute motifs. Based on three sketches drawn in 1913, 1915, and 1917, this secretary was inspired by a type of lady's writing desk of the eighteenth century known as a *bonheur-du-jour*. It was not produced until 1921, when it was first exhibited at the Salon d'Automne in Paris. Known as the "Tibattant" secretary, it was made in various decorative woods and remained in the production catalogue until the firm closed after Ruhlmann's death in 1933.

Macassar ebony, ivory, and suede
Mark: Ruhlmann (stamped)
Height 44¼″ (113 cm)
Gift of COLLAB. 1976-227-1

Covered Jar, 1924
Maurice Marinot (French, 1882–1960)

22

One of the most celebrated glassmakers of the twentieth century, Maurice Marinot began his career as a painter and continued to paint during the two and a half decades he made glass. In 1911 he took up glassmaking through the offices of his friends, the brothers Viard, who operated a glasshouse at Bar-sur-Seine. He began by decorating glass with colored enamels, but from about 1919 to 1927, Marinot learned to blow his own glass and to decorate it in a variety of other techniques. Much of his glass of this period is characterized by the use of freely ascending bubbles, and the artist's control of this technique has never been equaled. In this jar the bubbles fizz upward in a perfectly even layer until they are finally concentrated in the spherical finial of the cover. In 1920 Marinot had written an article on the craft of glassblowing, which shows that he had early appreciated the problems of working the glass hot, in a malleable state, at the furnace and then cooling it to produce such effects: "If one loves glass one must desire humbly and tenaciously to know it. To be a glassman is not to trace lines or to put spots on glass . . . because there is no real knowledge of the material. To be a glassman is to blow the transparent material close to the blinding furnace, by the breath of your lips and by the tools of your craft, to work in the roasting heat and the smoke, your eyes full of tears, your hands burned and dirtied with coal dust . . . to rediscover in the brilliant immobility of the glass the life of the human breath."

Grayish, bubbled glass
Mark: marinot (etched)
Height 10¾" (27.3 cm)
Gift of Mlle Florence Marinot. 67-98-15a,b

Bowl, 1924
François-Emile Décorchemont (French, 1880–1971)

François-Emile Décorchemont, like Maurice Marinot, began his career as a painter and continued to paint throughout his life. About 1903, probably influenced by the glass artist Albert Dammouse, he created his first glasswares, which were executed in *pâte de verre* (glass paste), a technique in which the body is built up in a mold from a paste of powdered glass and metallic oxides and fired. Although his earliest pieces were small and not typical of the medium, Décorchemont became France's principal artist in the development of this technique. From about 1907, using powdered crystal that he cast by the lost-wax process and polished, he obtained true glass pastes, thick and translucent, which sometimes took on the appearance of hard stones. From such early works with their rich Art Nouveau ornaments, Décorchemont by 1920 had turned to much plainer shapes, sometimes angular in outline, decorated with geometric patterns of circles and triangles, and stylized flowers. This bowl, with its etched rosette decoration, is typical of that period and of the Art Deco style, named for the 1925 Exposition Internationale des Arts Décoratifs et Industriels Modernes in Paris. There Décorchemont's glass was exhibited in several pavilions, including those of Emile-Jacques Ruhlmann and the Groupe des Artisans Français Contemporains, and the artist was described as being at the full height of his creative abilities, synthesizing all the "nobility" of craftsmanship.

From the Décorchemont notebooks, now in the Musée des Arts Décoratifs in Paris, this bowl can be precisely dated to October 1925. The model (number 229), noted as "frieze of three rosettes," was actually designed in 1924, and twelve examples were produced in 1924–25. These were sold by the Paris firm of Rouard, which had handled Décorchemont's work since 1907.

Pâte de verre (glass paste)
Mark: A286 (etched)
Diameter 6 7/16″ (16.4 cm)
Gift of Mrs. Christine P. Rosengarten
69-197-2

Footed Cup, c. 1926
Josef Hoffmann (Austrian, 1870–1956)

26 A brass version of this silver cup was published in a 1926 article celebrating the Wiener Werkstätte, a communal workshop of designers and craftsmen in Vienna. Their metalwares were described "as modeled on the English example. The material, in flat, lightly bowed sheets is formed together in that Empire shape most nearly reminiscent of Greek vases and jugs." The reference to English products is noteworthy, since the Werkstätte had been founded partly on the model—if not the aesthetic—of the workshops of the Arts and Crafts movement. In the Werkstätte's founding manifesto, Josef Hoffmann drew on the theories of John Ruskin and William Morris, preaching the virtues of the craft aesthetic as a redemptive force in an industrialized society: "The boundless evil, caused by shoddy mass-produced goods, and by the uncritical imitation of earlier styles, is like a tidal wave sweeping across the world. The machine has largely replaced the hand and the business-man has supplanted the craftsman. Our guiding principle is function, utility our first condition, and our strength must lie in good proportions and the proper treatment of material." Throughout the 1920s the Werkstätte produced furniture, metalwork, ceramics, glassware, wallpapers, textiles, bookbindings, and graphics, which were sold in branch shops in European cities and New York. By 1920 the geometric style of the workshop's early designs had grown more decorative and fanciful. Balancing the restraint of a simple, fluted shape with the extravagant, curled handles and the densely hammered and chased surface, Hoffmann here displayed the virtuoso qualities of hand labor, qualities that were appreciated more by an affluent international market than by the "ordinary citizens" whom the Wiener Werkstätte had been founded to serve.

Made by the Wiener Werkstätte, Vienna (1903–1932)
Chased and hammered silver
Marks: JH [for Josef Hoffmann], WW [for Wiener Werkstätte], Made in Austria, Austrian guaranty mark for the .9 silver standard used after 1922 (stamped)
Height 7¼″ (18.5 cm)
Purchased with funds contributed by COLLAB and Mr. and Mrs. Adolph G. Rosengarten, and the Fiske Kimball Fund
1981-89-1

Vase, 1926
Claudius Linossier (French, 1893–1953)

Working virtually alone in his workshop in Lyons, Claudius Linossier created some 4,000 pieces of decorated metalwork over a thirty-year period. Having followed a traditional apprenticeship in metalwork and enameling for six years, some of it in the large Paris workshops of Cardeilhac and, for a short time, Jean Dunand (when the latter's principal work was still as a coppersmith), he returned to Lyons, his birthplace, in 1920 to open his own shop. There he painstakingly hammered metal sheets into plates, bowls, and vases; decorated them with encrustations of other metals; and created patinas to unify and color each design, using hammer and furnace as his primary tools. His was an art of metal alone, his objective "to achieve painting on metal, without having recourse to enamel." Through experimentation he developed his own methods for achieving the colorations he required, employing copper, brass, nickel silver, and silver, one metal over another. Linossier quickly gained a reputation as a decorative craftsman, and he showed his work at the 1925 Exposition Internationale des Arts Décoratifs in Paris, both independently, in the section of Art and Industries of Metal, and in the installations of other designers, collaborating with Emile-Jacques Ruhlmann on the furnishing of his Hôtel du Collectionneur. This vase, created the following year, is number 664 in the repertory of Linossier designs, a photoarchive developed by Linossier that documents some 3,600 of his pieces. The round, hammered-copper form with a variegated patina of red and black is decorated with a geometric, chevroned band of silver and a patinated copper that gives a golden effect; versions of this decoration appear on a number of vases of similar shape in various sizes listed in the photoarchive from the same period.

Patinated copper with silver overlays
Mark: Cl. Linossier 1926 (engraved)
Height 7⅝" (19.4 cm)

Purchased: Haney Foundation Fund
74-60-1

Armchair, 1927
Ludwig Mies van der Rohe (German, 1886–1969)

The notion of functionalism, which judges aesthetics in terms of honest expression of materials and structure and of utility, not decoration, dates to the mid-nineteenth century, but the works connected with the Bauhaus, the German design school founded in 1919, are usually seen as its paradigms. This chair, with its simple geometric forms and polished seamless steel tubing, stands as an archetypal Bauhaus product, although its designer, the architect Ludwig Mies van der Rohe, did not join the staff (as director) until 1930. Cantilevered steel chairs had been produced earlier, but in line with the Bauhaus ideal of the interaction of art and technology, Mies investigated further the possibilities of steel tubing and in 1927 received a patent covering his use of its spring quality. The principle's earliest application was in chairs of this design, produced with and without arms and fitted with leather sling backs and seats. They were first used in the apartment house Mies designed for the Weissenhof experimental garden city in Stuttgart in 1927; versions with lacquered cane seats were exhibited later that year in Berlin. The chair has been continuously in production since 1927, the first manufacturer being the Berliner Metallgewerbe Joseph Müller (1927–30); it has been produced since 1931 by Thonet and was among the Mies furniture revived by Knoll after the war, when the architect had become established in America. Mies created furniture for his buildings, and the some fifteen models that went into production (all essentially designed from 1927 to 1931) continued to be used in his interiors throughout his career. Like this design and his better-known Barcelona chair (1929), they all employ similar elegant lines and materials that fittingly mark the spaces of his modernist buildings.

Chrome-plated steel and lacquered caning
Height 31″ (78.7 cm)
Gift of COLLAB in memory of Roland
Gallimore. 1978-116-1

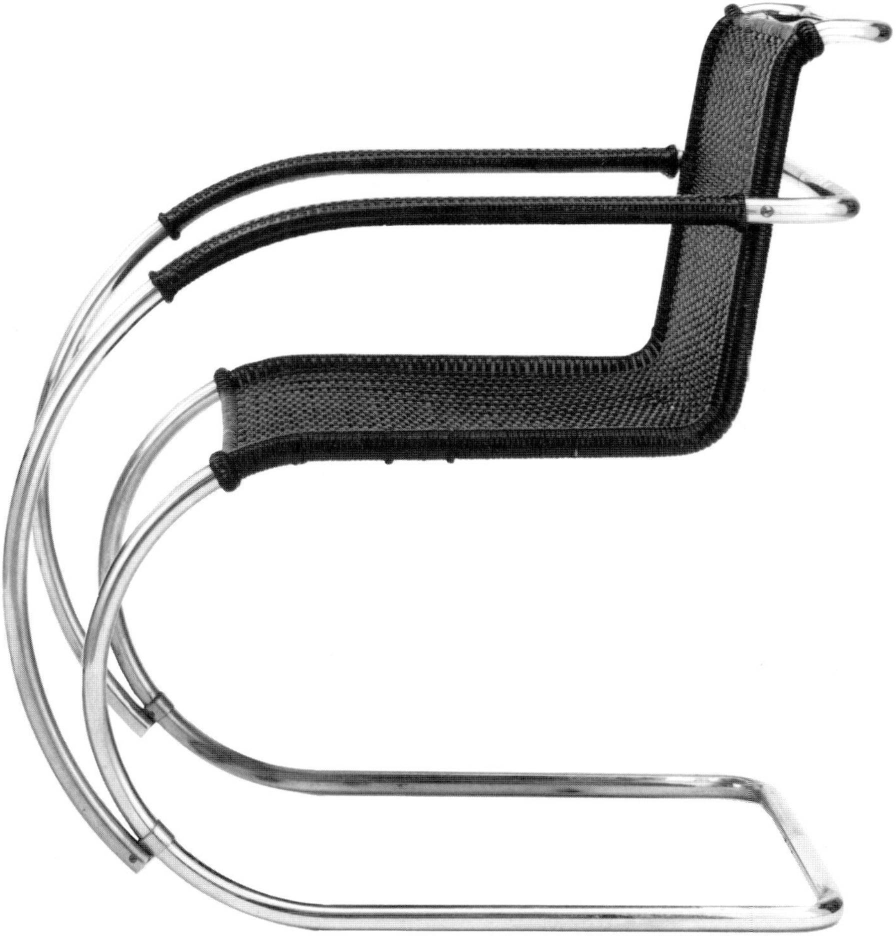

Panel, 1925–30
Jean Dunand (French, born Switzerland, 1877–1942)

32 Trained as a sculptor, Jean Dunand was working and exhibiting in Paris as a metalsmith when in 1912 he learned the process of Oriental lacquer from a Japanese craftsman. He first used lacquer to enhance his vases, but after the First World War, having developed the technique further, he added a cabinetry shop to make small objects, furniture, panels, and screens, which he decorated with lacquer. As commissions came in, he employed scores of workers to follow the tedious procedures of the age-old lacquer technique; as many as thirty or forty applications of the natural resin were required to achieve a brilliant, durable lacquer surface, and each coat took at least several days to harden before it could be burnished by hand and the next one applied.

His lacquer designs, often created in collaboration with other artists, vary from African and other exotic motifs in a flat, decorative style to astonishing cubistic abstractions and realistic portraiture. For the 1925 Paris exposition, Dunand conceived and furnished an entire interior: a lacquered and gilded smoking room for a French embassy. The next year, for his friend the milliner Agnes, he decorated a salon in the same fashion. This panel of the martyr Saint Agnes in prayer, with the Lamb of God before her and the sacrificial altar beyond, may relate to that commission and allude to the modiste's name, for another panel with a woman and a lamb adorns a mirror that Dunand designed for her salon. Dunand colored his lacquer with natural earths (the reds here are derived from cinnabar) and used iron oxides to create his black and silvery gray tones. He often embedded other materials in lacquer—powdered eggshell for light tones; mother-of-pearl; and metallic foils and flakes, as seen here on the hands and face—and ornamented the surfaces with engraving.

Lacquer with metallic flakes and foil over
cloth and composition board
Signed: JEAN DUNAND
$32\frac{7}{8}$ x $22\frac{7}{16}$″ (83.5 x 57 cm)
Gift of the Rosenbach Company. 44-46-3

Pitcher, 1927
Kay Fisker (Danish, 1893–1965)

This pitcher, designed in 1927 by the architect Kay Fisker, was one of the earliest pieces of Danish silver to respond to the concept of functionalism as practiced at the German Bauhaus, and it was through such work, rather than architecture, that the modernist International style was most strongly realized in Denmark in the 1920s. With its simple outline and shiny surface from which all signs of handwork and decorative detail have been eliminated, the pitcher appears as if manufactured by machine although it was crafted by hand using standard techniques. The liveliness of its sophisticated profile, which was fully worked out on paper by the architect and then translated into metal by the silversmith, depends on the fluid line that unites rounded body, flat handle, and exaggerated lip into one plastic form. Fisker's earlier designs for the jeweler and silversmith A. Michelsen were shown in Paris at the 1925 Exposition des Arts Décoratifs, where the reports noted their "spirit of sobriety, selection, and purity." Between 1925 and 1928 Fisker designed several groups of silver for Michelsen, and although they do not consistently reflect the same concern for spare functionalism—others are elaborated with ornamental detail or recall Oriental and eighteenth-century models—the designs were essentially independent and had considerable influence on later silverwork in Denmark. Over the next decades Michelsen continued to employ noted architects (including Denmark's most famous, Arne Jacobsen) as designers of silver tablewares, and following Fisker's lead, they were responsible for introducing innovative forms into the company's products. It was not until after 1930 that the better-known Danish firm Georg Jensen took the modern approach that Fisker and Michelsen had pioneered.

Made by A. Michelsen, Copenhagen (established 1841), 1957
Silver
Marks: A MICHELSEN (in rectangle, crowned); L; G 9 KAY FISKER R (in circle) 1,5 L; STERLING DENMARK (in rectangle) (stamped)
Height 10 7/16" (26.5 cm)
Gift of Mrs. Albert M. Greenfield. 72-101-3

Armchair, c. 1933
Alvar Aalto (Finnish, 1898–1976)

This high-back armchair, one of only several examples known, is a variant of the "standard" chair number 31 (see cover) that Alvar Aalto designed for the Paimio Sanatorium between 1930 and 1933 and that has remained in almost continuous production ever since. Built as a free cantilever, it has a seat and back formed from one long, curving panel of springy, molded plywood suspended between two U-shaped loops of thicker, laminated strips. The idea of the cantilever seat in an open frame came to Aalto through the chair designs of the Bauhaus architects Marcel Breuer and Ludwig Mies van der Rohe, but in its translation from tubular steel to bent wood, Aalto's chair was wholly innovative in its form and in the technology required to produce it. It was also equally rational but more "human," as Aalto noted in 1940: "Tubular and chromium surfaces are good solutions technically, but psychophysically these materials are not good for the human being. The sanatorium needed furniture that should be light, flexible, easy to clean, and so on. After extensive experimentation in wood, the flexible system was discovered and a method and material combined to produce furniture that was better for the human touch and more suitable as the general material for the long and painful life in a sanatorium."

The Paimio furniture brought Aalto international recognition when it was exhibited at the Triennale in Milan and at the Fortnum and Mason department store in London, both in 1933. The public demand for it was so extensive that an English company, Finmar, was founded to import Aalto furniture, and a Finnish company, Artek, was established by Aalto and others in 1935 to produce and market the designs, as it continues to do even to this day.

Made by Huonekalu-ja Rakennustyötendas Oy, Turku (established 1910)
Laminated birch, birch plywood, and leather
Height 37½″ (95.2 cm)

Purchased with funds contributed by COLLAB in honor of Cynthia W. Drayton, and the Fiske Kimball Fund. 1985-67-1

Vase, 1935
Vicke Lindstrand (Swedish, 1904–1983)

As a result of the crusade of the Swedish Association of Arts and Crafts for the beautification of everyday objects through the employment of artists in industry, two painters, Simon Gate and Edward Hald, joined the Orrefors glassworks in 1916 and 1917 and brought about a revitalization that led to great acclaim for the firm at the 1925 Paris exposition. In 1928 a third artist-designer, the sculptor Vicke Lindstrand, was brought to the glassworks and there worked in the innovative Orrefors community, which encouraged a reciprocal relationship between designer and craftsman. Orrefors, Lindstrand would later remark, is "inadequately described as a glassworks. It is really a cult in glass. . . . We have gone to live and work together at Orrefors, striving for the truest forms of expression in our exquisite medium. . . . We stand beside the man at the emery wheel who adds to the weighty modern pieces that supreme pictorial engraving which brings out their fundamental, mystical qualities. . . . We stand beside the furnaces and try to give the glassblowers the feel of what we are seeking."

In this engraved vase, known as "The Pearl Diver," Lindstrand created an imaginative underwater scene of a single, suspended diver, exploiting the undulating rhythms of the interior of the thick, refractive glass to convey a sense of movement and introducing bubbles for narrative ends. The formalized muscular figure, a heroic type used elsewhere by Lindstrand (and in many images of the 1930s), is deeply cut in the wall of the vessel, the depth of the engraving varying greatly as it defines the broad forms of the figure or the details of its outline. "The Pearl Diver," in production from 1935 to about 1963, was one of the most popular designs produced by Orrefors during that period.

Engraved by Arthur Roos (active 1924–74)
Made by Orrefors Glasbruk (established 1898), 1948
Clear glass with wheel-engraved decoration

Mark: ORREFORS LINDSTRAND 1343 B. 5 AR. (etched)
Height 11⅛" (28.4 cm)
Gift of Mrs. Henry W. Breyer, Sr. 62-84-25

Covered Tureen, 1937
Jean Puiforcat (French, 1897–1945)

The official guide to the 1937 Paris Exposition Internationale, which had as its theme "Arts and Crafts in Modern Life," noted that the objects exhibited "have been conceived according to a new style: no more cubism, but a return to the curved or at least non-rigid line." Designed for the exposition by Jean Puiforcat, France's most important twentieth-century silversmith, this tureen exemplifies both the return to fluid lines in the 1930s and Puiforcat's own firm belief that "the circle, which explains the entire world, is the ideal figure, and the curve, which approaches it, is more noble than the straight line." If perfect forms were his goal, mathematics and the harmonious relationships of the golden section were the means he used to achieve them, working out his designs on paper in geometric drawings that he called "harmonic sketches." A full-scale drawing that has remained in the Puiforcat archives in Paris documents how the angles, arcs, and ratios of this tureen were generated mathematically, but his work transcends dry rationality and expresses the visual excitement he found in designing silver and combining it with ivory, rock crystal, fine wood, and other materials. Avoiding surface decoration or any element that would interrupt the sweep of this broadly curved silver ellipse, Puiforcat set it off in the middle with a bold band of blue hematite spheres. "The play of light that one achieves in organizing the surfaces of silver, in giving it different heights," he said, "is sufficient to amuse the eye and, moreover, has the advantage of emphasizing the essential qualities of the material itself."

Silver and hematite
Signed: JEAN E PUIFORCAT FRANCE
Marks: EP (in diamond, twice), French guaranty mark for the .95 silver standard used after 1838 (three times) (stamped)

Diameter 11¾" (30 cm)
Purchased. 48-70-1a,b

Tea Cart, 1936
Alvar Aalto (Finnish, 1898–1976)

Number 98 in the catalogue of Artek, this celebrated design consists of two wide strips of laminated wood, each bent into a closed curve, to which two trays have been attached to form shelves. Two wheels made of wooden disks are fixed at one end. Aalto's first idea for the cart appeared as a design for a small serving table, one of six entries he submitted on September 9, 1929, to the Thonet-Mundus furniture company in Berlin, which had announced a large international competition for new models. Although Aalto did not win a prize in the competition, his entry, which was designed with runners like a sled, eventually matured into this small tea trolley of 1936 and a larger version of 1937, two of the earliest models offered by Artek. From 1930, working with Otto Korhonen, the manufacturer of his furniture in Turku, Finland, Aalto resolved the technical problems inherent in producing the revolutionary form of the closed circular frame by employing laminated wood, which is extremely strong and pliable enough to be used for complicated bends and shapes. When the tea cart and other examples of Aalto's furniture were first exhibited at the Museum of Modern Art, New York, in 1938, it was the designer's use of this material that was considered distinctive: "Aalto's thorough knowledge of the various properties of wood guides his imagination in putting them to work . . . under the direction of his unique esthetic sensibility. In his furniture, the audacious manipulation of wood might be thought bravura were it not always justified by the physical properties of the material. As in his architecture, Aalto's designs are a result of the same combination of sound construction, suitability to use and sense of style."

Made by Huonekalu-ja Rakennustyötendas Oy, Turku (established 1910) for Artek Oy Ab (established Helsinki 1935)
Laminated birch, glass, and cork
Height $23\frac{9}{16}''$ (59.9 cm)

Purchased with funds contributed by COLLAB in honor of Cynthia W. Drayton, and the Fiske Kimball Fund. 1985-67-3

Vase, 1939
Edvin Ohrström (Swedish, born 1906)

Edvin Ohrström, a sculptor by training, was hired by Orrefors as a glass designer in 1936 and within a year expanded the firm's methods of manufacturing colored glass, for which it had become celebrated during the 1920s. Working with Vicke Lindstrand, he developed the Ariel technique, which employs the manipulation of air bubbles within the body of the glass. When used in combination with Orrefors's *graal* technique, the Ariel process calls for a pattern to be sandblasted into one layer of glass and encased within another, creating colorful decorative patterns with fluid lines and shimmering channels of air. The smooth, thick mass of this vase encases the heroic forms of horse, bull, and matador; through the very transparency of the glass, the three combatants remain always in view, locked in perpetual battle. Ohrström's Ariel designs were shown in the 1937 Exposition Internationale in Paris and again, in 1939, at the Swedish Pavilion at the New York World's Fair, from which this vase was originally purchased. The pavilion displayed the largest collection of industrial arts that Sweden had yet shown in America and, according to the guide, represented the culmination of Sweden's "20-year campaign for aesthetic design and high quality mass production at a price within the reach of all." Ohrström remained at Orrefors until 1958, creating, in addition to ornamental works in this technique, tableware for daily use and monumental windows and glass sculpture.

Made by Orrefors Glasbruk (established 1898)
Clear and colored layered glass
Marks: Sweden, Orrefors 1939, Ariel No 94, Edvin Ohrstrom (engraved)

Height $7\frac{15}{16}$" (20.2 cm)
Gift of Mrs. Christine P. Rosengarten
69-197-1

Vase, c. 1938
Svend Hammershøj (Danish, 1873–1948)

46 Inspired by Chinese ceramics, the simple form of this mat white vase is enlivened by its shallowly reeded surface, random splatter pattern, accidental crackle caused by the firing process, and black banding at the neck. This monumental piece was produced in the late 1930s by the firm of Herman A. Kähler after designs by Svend Hammershøj, along with a number of other vases, urns, and bowls that shared its style and technique. This series was very different from the bolder, more exuberant ceramics with brighter glazes and applied naturalistic ornament that the artist designed in the 1920s, when his work still revealed the influence of the Art Nouveau style of the Danish potter Thorvald Bindesbøll. Early in the century Bindesbøll had encouraged Hammershøj, already a successful painter, to collaborate with craftsmen and manufacturers, and throughout his career Hammershøj was to design ceramics, glass, silver, and leatherwork for industry while continuing to paint. By 1902 he was working with the Bing & Grøndahl porcelain factory, and in 1905–6 he became the first Danish artist to design for the glass industry, creating for the Holmegaards glassworks the "Margrethe" stemware service, which remained in production until 1960. Hammershøj designed silverwares for the firms of Holger Kyster and A. Michelsen in very personal styles that include strange, undulating sculptural forms that look as if molded in clay and naturalistic ornamentation that recalls his Art Nouveau beginnings.

Made by Herman A. Kähler, Naestved (established 1839)
Glazed, high-fired earthenware
Marks: HAK (incised and painted), Danmark (impressed)

Height 12¼″ (31.2 cm)
Purchased: Gertrude Schemm Binder Fund. 74-62-1

Sources of Quotations and Further Reading

Alvar Aalto Furniture. Cambridge, Mass., 1985.

K. Berling. *Meissen China*. Meissen, 1910. Reprint: New York, 1972.

Florence Camard. *Ruhlmann: Master of Art Deco*. New York, 1984.

Victor Champier. "Le Castel Béranger et M. Hector Guimard." *Revue des Arts Décoratifs*, vol. 19 (January 1899), pp. 1–10.

R. J. Charleston. "The Glass of Maurice Marinot." *Victoria and Albert Museum Bulletin*, vol. 1, no. 3 (July 1965), pp. 1–8.

Encyclopédie des arts décoratifs et industriels modernes au XXème siecle. 12 vols. Paris, 1925. Reprint: New York, 1977.

Ludwig Glaeser. *Ludwig Mies van der Rohe: Furniture* . . . . New York, 1977.

Hector Guimard. "An Architect's Opinion of 'L'Art Nouveau.'" *Architectural Record*, vol. 12 (May 1902), pp. 127–33.

Philip Gustafson. "The Glassmakers of Småland Woods." *Arts & Decoration*, vol. 50, no. 3 (June 1939), pp. 16–17, 47.

Ludwig Hevesi. *Altkunst-Neukunst, Wien 1894–1908*. Vienna, 1909.

Esbjørn Hiort. *Modern Danish Silver*. New York, 1954.

Houston, Institute for the Arts, Rice University. *Art Nouveau: Belgium, France*. March 26–June 27, 1976.

Jean Puiforcat: Orfèvre Sculpteur. Paris, 1951.

Josef Hoffmann: Architect and Designer, 1870–1956. New York, 1981.

Johannes Just. *Meissen Porcelain of the Art Nouveau Period*. Cincinnati, 1983.

Lyons, Musée des Beaux-Arts. *Claudius Linossier, Dinandier (1893–1953)*. 1979.

New York, The Museum of Modern Art. *Aalto*. March 1938.

Max Osborn. "Die Modernen Wohn-räume im Waren-haus von A. Wertheim zu Berlin." *Deutsche Kunst und Dekoration*, vol. 11 (March 1903), pp. 259–68.

Paris, Galerie du Luxembourg. *Jean Dunand, Jean Goulden*. May–July 1973.

Paris, Musée des Arts Décoratifs. *Art Deco 1925*. September 30–October 31, 1975.

Helmut Ricke and Ulrich Gronert. *Glas in Schweden: 1915–1960*. Munich, 1986.

Eduard F. Sekler. *Josef Hoffmann: The Architectural Work*. Princeton, 1985.

"Die Wiener Werkstätte." *Dekorative Kunst*, vol. 34 (1925–26), pp. 220–25.

Alan Windsor. *Peter Behrens, Architect and Designer*. New York, 1981.